An ELEGY on the DEATH of a MAD DOG.

WRITTEN
By
Dr GOLDSMITH

PICTURED
By
R. CALDECOTT

SUNG By Master BILL PRIMROSE

IN MEMORY OF TOBY

 Grolier Educational Corporation

Good people all, of every sort,
　　Give ear unto my song;
And if you find it wondrous short,
　　It cannot hold you long.

In Islington there lived a man,
    Of whom the world might say,
That still a godly race he ran,

4

When ever he went

to pray.

A kind and gentle heart he had.
To comfort friends and foes;
The naked every day he clad.

When he put on
his clothes

And in that town a dog was found,

As many dogs there be—

Both mongrel,   puppy,   whelp,

and hound,

And curs of low degree,

The dog and man at first were friends;

But, when a pique began,

The dog, to gain some private ends,

Went mad, and bit the man.

Around from all
the neighbouring streets

The wondering neighbours ran;

And swore the dog had lost his wits,
To bite so good a man.

The wound it seem'd both sore and sad
    To every christian eye;

And while they swore the dog was mad

They swore the man would die.

21

But soon a wonder came to light,
That show'd the rogues they lied—

The man recover'd of the bite;

The dog it was that died.